Thinking of You

To: _____

From: _____

The gift of God
is eternal life.
(John 3:16)

Unless otherwise indicated,
all Scripture quotations are taken from
the *King James Version* of the Bible.

ISBN O-937580-43-0
The Trajectory Of Faith

Set up and printed 1985
Published by LeSEA Publishing Company
P.O. Box 12
South Bend, Indiana 46624

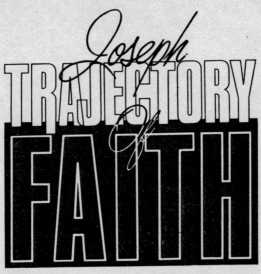

Dr. Lester Sumrall

PUBLICATION

CONTENTS

CONTENTS

1

THE TRAJECTORY BOMB

I was flying across the Pacific Ocean in a giant jet aircraft. We came down in Guam to disembark some passengers and take on others. We were ready to fly to Honolulu, when there came an announcement from the captain saying, "Look out the left side of your window quickly, please." We looked out just in time to see something splash into the water. He said, "We were delayed because that is a projectile shot from the Edwards Air Base in California, some ten thousand miles away, and it hit the target here within a one mile range." That is what we call trajectory—shooting an object into the air and plotting its course to a perfect target.

I received a telephone call from a church saying, "Would you please pray for us? The pastor has announced he is going to give up the church, leave the ministry, and close the church." The church had about a thousand people. You see, the pastor was disturbed about the middle of life and not the end!

When you begin your spiritual life in Jesus Christ and you are born again, God puts the spiritual power inside of you for you to reach your target—your heavenly home, the new Jerusalem. Then it is up to you to be sure that in your great arch of life that you are right on target for the end of it.

Almost all the preachers that began preaching when I did are one of two places—either dead or in a retirement home sitting in a rocking chair. I want to live out the full measure of my days. I am determined that in the end of this projection of life I shall be right on target with God!

Between the beginning of your spiritual life and the end of your life, the devil tries to discourage you; he tries to beat you down; he tries to get you to stop; he tries to get you to go back. The devil does everything he can to keep you off God's target. If you will determine from the beginning that you are going to live on target with God, there are not enough devils to keep you off target!

2

JOSEPH
A TRAJECTORY
OF FAITH

Shall we look at a Biblical example of a man on course—a man who was successful on his trajectory of faith? Genesis 37:2 says, "These are the generations of Jacob. Joseph, being seventeen years old, was feeding the flock with his brethren; and the lad was with the sons of Bilhah, and with the sons of Zilpah, his father's wives: and Joseph brought unto his father their evil report."

SHUNNING EVIL

The first indication of spiritual power in Joseph was that he did not join in with his brothers' wickedness. There are people who go to jail for being present when a crime is committed. Joseph brought back to his father news that he had some bad sons. If that was all Joseph ever did, I would call him a tattletale.

JOSEPH GETS A COLORED COAT

Joseph's story worsens in the next verse, "Israel loved Joseph more than all his children, because he was the son of his old age: and he made him a coat of many colours."

We would say Joseph was a spoiled brat. That coat was the beginning of his troubles. It is so wrong for a father to love one of his sons more than another.

Joseph was now a young man with a couple of strikes against him. The first thing was his reporting of evil. The next thing was his father's showing too much affection for him. There was bound to be trouble in that house. Jacob not only loved and kissed him a lot, but made him a brilliant, multicolored coat. That is the most thoughtless thing a father could do. What boy needs a striped coat? Colored coats go to girls, not boys.

A STRANGE DREAM

There was hatred brewing in that family. Verse 4 says that "His brethren, they hated him, and could not speak peaceably to him." Joseph was miserable. There were two reasons: he told on his brothers and had a pretty coat.

Verse 5 is where our interest in Joseph begins. "Joseph dreamed a dream, and he told it to his brethren: and they hated him yet the more."

In Genesis 37:6-7, he said to his brothers, "Hear, I pray you, this dream which I have dreamed: For, behold, we were binding sheaves in the field, and, lo, my sheaf arose, and also stood upright; and, behold, your sheaves stood round about, and made obeisance to my sheaf."

Any spiritual phenomena that exalts you will get you in trouble with the rest of your family. You just become more spiritual than other members of your family and they will call you "preacher" or "deacon."

This young man Joseph dreamed of his destiny. That will also get you into trouble with the family, especially if you are the kid brother. Here was a younger brother who told his older brothers, "I had a dream. We were all in the field bringing in the wheat with the sheaves bundled up. My sheaves stood upright and all your sheaves knelt down and did obeisance. They worshipped me."

Now if you want trouble in a home, just let one of them ask for worship. They will not give him worship; they will give him hell.

It made his brothers more angry. It even gave his overindulgent father some concern.

A WORSE DREAM

Joseph dreamed again and this time his mother and father were bowing down to him. Genesis 37 gives us the story. The brethren went to feed their father's flock in Shechem, which is in Samaria. Jacob's home was probably near Hebron. The brothers were feeding the flocks fifty to seventy miles north. There is good grazing land in Shechem and not many hills. Jacob said, "Joseph, Do not thy brethren feed the flock in Shechem? Come, and I will send thee unto them."

Joseph responded to him, "Here am I." Jacob directed him, "Go I pray thee, see whether it be well with thy brethren, and well with the flocks; and bring me word again..."

Joseph went through the vale of Hebron by Bethlehem, Jerusalem, Bethel, and came to Shechem. That is rough territory to travel through.

In Shechem a certain man found Joseph

wandering in the fields and asked him who he was looking for. The lad responded, "I seek for my brothers. Tell me, I pray thee, where do they feed the flock?" The stranger's answer came, "They departed here. I heard them say that they would go to Dothan." This area is another thirty or forty miles further north and back toward the west.

HATE GIVES BIRTH TO MURDER

When the older brothers saw Joseph afar off, before he came near them, they conspired to slay their own younger brother. They said to one another, "Here comes the dreamer! Come, therefore, and let us slay him."

Joseph was a young man born into a religious home. When he was seventeen years old, he had his first identity with God. He hated evil and would not go along with it. There are still some people like that. Thank God for them. Then he saw a vision of his life. He saw his future life at the age of seventeen. So did Oral

Roberts; so did Lester Sumrall. I saw a vision at seventeen in Panama City, Florida: I knew what I was to do the rest of my life.

COAT OF SENTIMENTALITY

Joseph saw his life, but his father became overanxious. He gave Joseph a beautiful coat, I call it the coat of sentimentality.

Now God does not like sentiment. This multicolored frock was a coat of sentimentality.

When Joseph came bringing food to his brothers they said, "Let us kill him." They took his coat, and he never got it back. They said, "We will kill him after we eat his food." They dropped Joseph into a pit while they ate the food he had brought.

SELLING GOLD FOR SILVER

In the meantime, their country cousins, the Ishmaelites, the children of Abraham by Hagar, came by and Joseph's brothers said, "Hey, cousins, where are you going?" The Ishmaelites answered, "Going to Egypt for commerce." The brothers had an immediate response. "Well, we have some merchandise—a boy!" They did not even tell the merchants he was their brother. The traders queried, "Well, how much do you want for him?" The response came, "Twenty pieces of silver." That was the price of a slave. Can you imagine selling solid gold for silver? That boy was gold, and they sold him for a little silver. As they pulled him out of the hole, they taunted him... "Go dream your dreams, boy. We're rid of you."

But there are some people you cannot get rid of; they keep turning up. With God's hand on their lives you cannot do anything about it; they just keep turning up.

Joseph found himself, with his hands tied behind him, marching toward Egypt as a slave. He said, "You know, I used to wear a colored coat. Now I do not even have a coat.

Joseph arrived in Egypt as a slave. There was so much that could have happened to him, emotionally and spiritually. Hate could have filled his heart.

But what happened to his disposition? Did he get angry at his brothers? Did he get angry at everybody? Did he curse the Egyptians and hate them? What happened to Joseph in his strange trajectory of life from his affectionate parents to a pit and then to Egyptian slavery?

The same experience can happen to two people and one will go up and the other one will go down. God is not to blame. Your whole life depends on what is on the inside of you. How do you react to trouble? How do you react to sorrow? How do you react to adverse circumstances? Do not blame God! You have the choice.

3

A SLAVE PROSPERS

Possibly all the way to Egypt the Ishmaelites mistreated him.

In Egypt the slave masters must have said, "Boy, you must have been bad to be sold like this." Standing on the block, the auctioneer announced that a young male slave was for sale. All the Egyptians were looking at him and said, "He is a foreigner. He cannot even speak our language. He is not worth much, but he does have a good body. He can work."

A man named Potiphar outbid the others and bought Joseph to be a servant.

Potiphar was Chief of State of the armies of Egypt. He was probably a five-star general. Pharaoh had him as the chief of his bodyguard to protect him. He had a very influential position.

Joseph had no hope of ever seeing his father and mother again. There was certainly no hope of ever wearing his colored coat anymore. He was all finished. He was a slave in a foreign country.

What did Joseph do? He learned the language of Egypt and went to work. That is what most people run from, but work is the most satisfying thing in the world. In Potiphar's house he learned the Egyptian language and began to take care of his master's business. Every week he would get a promotion because the Egyptians would steal from the master, but Joseph would not. Honesty and integrity made a difference. Everything Joseph touched in Potiphar's house prospered. He was elevated until he became the master servant. A foreigner had become the top man.

Nothing can hold you down in this world if you will take charge of every opportunity and work hard.

When my family and I returned from living in the Philippines, we had nothing. I had given my life to missions all over the world. I did not own a folding chair. Then God said, "I am ready to bless you." I was past fifty, but that was not too old to receive God's blessing. God has given our ministry two television stations, a radio station, a beautiful new church, a Bible college, a Christian school, and the list goes on.

The desire of my heart was to preach to millions and take one million souls to heaven by television. Every day through our television ministry we reach six, or seven, or eight million people. The PTL network has over 2000 cable outlets. The Trinity Network has over 500 towns and cities. I am on both of these networks twice a day. Besides this, we have our own satellite uplink station. I teach by satellite to many churches from California to New York on Monday nights and every Sunday

morning I teach a Bible class to the whole
nation by satellite and by television stations.

I believe that is what Jesus can do when
you are a nobody and a nothing. Jesus
can bless you, but you have to have the
right spirit inside. You must love people.
You have to forgive people. You have to
care for people.

THE COAT OF HUMAN AUTHORITY

When Joseph was honored as chief servant, do you know what Potiphar did? He
gave Joseph a coat. It was his second coat
and it was the coat of human authority.
All the servants in Potiphar's house said,
"Wow! Look at that coat!" Nobody had
a coat like Joseph's coat. It was the top of
the line. It was the only one made by that
pattern and Joseph wore it. The man who
ruled the house wore the coat of human
authority or achievement. Joseph earned
that coat with his own initiative. It was a
coat earned by hard work. Joseph rose up
in his own might and his own intelligence,

and earned himself a coat of human authority. After Joseph became the head of the house, Potiphar greatly increased in wealth and riches. The prosperity came in so fast that the bookkeepers could not keep the records current. (Genesis 39:5-6)

While Potiphar was away fighting with the army, his beautiful wife observed this stately young man who was just over twenty years of age. Joseph carried himself as a leader. He spoke to the servants as a leader. Joseph was the boss and the servants feared him. He could advance their positions or leave them where they were. Joseph walked with dignity and strength with his new coat.

Potiphar's beautiful wife said, "I would like to have that boy." She dressed in her magnificent silks and dabbed on intriguing perfumes, and called to Joseph, "Come here." Being a servant he had to come. She said, "You are going to make love with me and we are going to have a great time." Joseph was a very logical person, not emotional. He said, "Now listen, my mistress, I was sold here as a slave and a foreigner. I learned your language and worked for your husband. He is now one of the richest men in the land of Egypt. I multiplied all the things that he had until he has riches that he cannot count. There is only one thing that he has not given to me; that is you. I could not violate the trust of a man that I love as I do your husband and my master. I cannot touch you. I will serve you. I will bring you anything you need, but I will not go to bed with you.''

The Bible says that Potiphar's wife continually enticed him. (Genesis 37:7-20) Everytime it was convenient, she tried to get to him.

One day her passions were so wild that she grabbed him and took hold of his coat and held on. Her grasp was so strong that Joseph raised his arms and slipped out of the coat. He exclaimed, ''Mistress, you can have my coat, but you cannot have my virtue.''

LUST AND HATE

Lust and hate are twins. They sleep in

the same bed. The people who lust after
you will also hate you. Many marriages
end in divorce when lust turns to hate.

Potiphar's wife saw the empty coat and
not the man. The lust turned into the bit-
terness of deep anger. She sat and cried
because she could not get the man she
wanted.

When Potiphar arrived home she fab-
ricated the biggest lie of her life. "Oh,
honey, see this coat?" "Yes, what is it doing here? That's Joseph's coat." "Oh,
yes, he is one thing to you, but when you
are gone, he is something else. He came
running in here like a wild man and took
off his coat and was going to go to bed
with me. I screamed and yelled and
fought him off. Finally help came and he
ran away. He ought to be dead."

It is amazing how a sin-filled woman
can influence an intelligent man to do the
wrong thing. If you want a man really
mad, touch his wife. You can steal his
money and he may forgive you, but do

not touch his wife! This general of the army was furiously angry and yelled. "I will chew him up and spit him out! Find him!" When the messenger located Joseph in his quarters, Potiphar fumed and demanded that he be put in the royal dungeon!

THE ROYAL JAIL

Joseph was now in the hole. If you think today's jails are bad, you should see the ancient Egyptian jails!

Young Joseph arrived in chains. He walked in and the prisoners asked, "What are you in here for?" He said, "For being a good man."

In a few days Joseph said, "Our jail is not very clean, and I have come to help clean it up." He began to clean out the spittoons of murderers and thieves. He began to sweep the floors for the meanest men in Egypt. When they needed something he said, "May I bring it to you?" They said, "Man, you are not a prisoner.

You are not a criminal. Why do you work so hard?" Joseph replied, "You need a little sunlight in this dark place. Those rats are annoying. The food is not very digestible. I will be the cook." He made clean food for the prisoners to enjoy. He made the prisoners work. The Bible says the prison superintendent made him the chief of the jail. The head of the prison could have all the time off he wanted for nobody wanted to leave because of Joseph. They were having a delightful time in prison because Joseph knew how to prosper. He knew how to make things go further; he knew how to make them more delicious. Egypt had never seen a jail like Joseph's jail. He lost his second coat, but he was not discouraged in his trajectory of faith.

4

THE VISION
DID NOT DIE

Joseph was in prison almost ten years. The devil taunted him saying, "You will die in here!" Joseph replied, "Devil, I want to tell you something. When I was seventeen years old, God showed me that my brothers would kneel down to me and they have not done that yet." Joseph was living with his first vision.

OF BREAD AND WINE

Two royal prisoners were thrown into the jail—the butler and the baker who served the wine and baked the bread for Pharaoh. Each of them had a dream while in prison. They became very sad. The butler said, "In my dream I saw a vine with three branches. It had ripe grapes and I pressed the juice into Pharaoh's cup." Joseph prayed and said, "Jehovah God can tell you. The three branches mean three days. In three days you will be back to serve the king."

The baker said in his dream he had three white baskets on his head full of meats, and the birds came and took the meat and ate it." Joseph responded, "In three days Pharaoh is going to hang you. The birds shall eat your flesh." Three days later it all came to pass.

To the butler, Joseph asked, "When you return to the palace, remember me." But the butler forgot.

Two years later (Genesis 41:1) the king began to dream. Pharaoh dreamed that he saw seven fat cows come up out of the Nile River. Then in his dream he saw seven lean and miserable cows come up out of the river. To his amazement, the lean cows ate the fat ones.

Then the king dreamed again and saw seven large, full ears of corn on one stalk. However, seven lean and blasted ears sprang up after them.

He saw in his dream that the thin and lean ears of corn ate up the fat ones. What a dream!

Pharaoh was terribly troubled. He called his magicians and astrologers. None could interpret the dreams.

The chief butler finally remembered that he had forgotten Joseph. Genesis 41:14 tells us that Pharaoh called for Joseph hastily. A royal guard ran down to the jail and said, "Is there a man named Joseph here?" "Yes, sir; just had a bath this morning and I am clean and ready to get out." His case was packed. He was expecting deliverance. He knew it had to come!

JOSEPH INTERPRETS
A ROYAL DREAM

Joseph departed the royal prison and soon stood before the king of the most powerful nation in existence. Pharaoh told his dream to the prisoner. He said, "There came up seven ears of good corn and seven ears of bad corn. The bad ones ate the good and were still lean. And there came seven fat cows and seven lean cows. The lean cows ate the fat cows and they were still lean. Why do I dream things like that?"

Joseph replied, "God will give you an answer."

Joseph said, "Jehovah God speaks to me, sir, that both dreams are the same; they are identical. You are going to have seven years of plenty in this land, and then you are going to have seven years of famine. Now sir, if you are wise, during these seven years of plenty you will gather vast amounts of grain and build great granaries for storage.

5

FROM PRISONER
TO PRIME MINISTER

Do you want me to prophesy? Our
President needs a Joseph more than he
needs anyone else. You know there are
famines in Africa and India. If America
misses one harvest in this country, hun-
dreds of millions would starve to death.
Russia continually has terrible droughts
and dreadful shortages. They cannot raise
sufficient food to feed their people.

ARE YOU THIRTY?

Joseph was thirty years old when he

stood before Pharaoh. That was the same age as Jesus when He started preaching. That was the age of David when he became king. Thirty is a number of destiny. Look at your life at thirty. From the time you are a baby until you are thirty, you are receiving. When you get to thirty, you start using. When you get to sixty, you start giving away because you do not need it any longer. You have three time periods in your life—getting, using, and giving.

Here Joseph stood at thirty years of age and said, "Oh King, if you are wise, build the largest granaries to store grain because the world will have a great famine after seven years." Pharaoh scratched his head and said, "I have no one as smart as you are; I will give you the job! In fact, I will make you next to me, the prime minister of Egypt." That is what you call instant success...out of a jail cell to the office of prime minister!

COAT OF DIVINE REVELATION

Do you know what Pharaoh did? He

gave Joseph a coat! I imagine Joseph said, "Sir, I do not want a special coat. I have already had two coats and they got me into a lot of trouble!" This third coat was different. The first coat represented the sentimentality of an indulgent father. The second coat represented human achievement of a dynamic youth grabbing for the whole world. The third coat came to him by divine revelation. Joseph did not do anything, but God spoke the revelation and used Joseph's lips to give it. You do not lose a coat that comes spiritually by divine revelation. Joseph lived to be 110 years old, but he never lost another coat. That coat was given by God.

6

THE TRAJECTORY
OF FORGIVENESS

When Pharaoh made Joseph prime minister of Egypt, he said, "Tomorrow night we shall have a royal banquet and the whole nation will rejoice over our new prime minister. You will announce your food program."

Joseph responded, "Thank you, your majesty. I have one request."

The monarch asked, "What is your request?"

"Is Potiphar still your chief of staff?"

Oh, yes, he is the bravest man in the nation.''

"And is his wife still living?"

"Do you know Potiphar?"

"Oh, yes, I knew them at one time. May I have them sit near me? I know I will be sitting at your right hand. Could I have them at my left hand? Both Potiphar and his wife?"

The Pharaoh replied. "I was going to let them sit at the head table, but if you want them next to you, you may have your desire."

Joseph replied to Pharaoh, "I do want Potiphar and his wife. I want his wife next to me, and Potiphar next to her."

The news that there was a new prime minister went through the nation like lightning. In honor of the event, Pharaoh was having a great ball and all the celebrities and noble people of the nation would be present at that great banquet.

There came a special messenger to Potiphar and his wife. They were to be the honored guests and sit by Joseph. Potipher's wife began to have delirium tremens as she looked at her husband and said, "You are going to die, too. You are the one who believed the lie I told and put Joseph in jail." They both had the shakes. They said, "Poor Joseph has been in jail ten years! He hates our guts. All he will have to do is stand up before the king and say, 'These two put me in jail for ten years and I did not do anything wrong.' " They said to each other, "We are dead! We are dead!"

Potiphar said, "What shall we do for him? What present can we give him?" They dressed in their very best finery and came to the banquet, fearing for their lives.

At the banquet, first came the emperor and his queen. There was great applause! Then Joseph was escorted in and seated by him. Next they brought out the chief of staff with his beautiful wife. She was given a seat by Joseph. Her hand was trembling, but Joseph put his hand on hers and said, "Darling, you look so pretty tonight and I am so glad to see you."

"What did you say, Joseph? I am so sorry for what I did..."

"Oh, do not say that. This is the night of great rejoicing! Let me tell you something. If it had not been for you, I would not have become prime minister. Thank you so very much."

Joseph patted her hand and consoled them both. No doubt Joseph embraced the chief of staff and said, "Sir, I will have you to run before my horses for me and tell the people that the prime minister is coming. I have already told the emperor that I will use you as my man of honor. You will go before me and say, 'Behold the prime minister!' I have given you a new position and I think you are a great man."

One of the greatest attributes in the world is forgiveness toward those people who have hurt you.

THE TRAJECTORY OF VISION

What was the secret of Joseph's greatness? It was his ability to stick with his original vision that God gave him. There are a lot of people who have lost their first vision because they hit on hard places. God says, "Do not quit. Do not abandon your vision. Life's road is littered with quitters because things got tough and things got hard. If you keep going, you will win, and there is nothing to keep you from winning if you keep going!"

FOOD STOCKPILE

For seven years Joseph made great domes and filled them with grain. He bought all of the available grain. The market was always his and he stored it and stored it, until he was almost a laughing stock, because he had millions and millions of tons of grain.

After seven years there was no rain. There was no harvest and the people had to start coming to Joseph to buy grain. Joseph sold it to them and gave all the money to the king. The king was the richest person on earth.

The next year there was no rain. Again there was no harvest. The people had no more money so he took their land. Now the king not only had all the money, he also owned all the land of Egypt.

Another year and still no rain nor harvest. The people sold their bodies to the king and became slaves. Whatever Joseph touched throughout life, whoever he worked for became successful and received the benefits.

7

THE VISION
FULFILLED

One day while Joseph's stewards were selling grain, they observed ten men together who wanted to purchase grain. The stewards said, "You are foreigners. We do not know whether we can sell grain to you or not. You will have to see the one who is in charge." Joseph had an Egyptian name, "Zaphnathpaaneah," and no one knew him by his Hebrew name any longer. Down the bright red carpet leading to his high seat, came ten men dressed in sheepskins. As they came, one of the Egyptian guards warned them, "Boys, you had better get low." They got on their knees and the Egyptian said, "If you want any grain you had better get lower." They came crawling on their elbows and knees, and the guard warned, "If you are smart, you will not look up either." Joseph thought to himself, "I know those boys. They are my brothers. That is just like my dream when I was seventeen years old. They are all bowing down to me."

You should always be careful. You can mistreat somebody to promote yourself, and you will wind up being the one who is down. If you push somebody down, that man might come up again and you will be down. As his brothers came up, Joseph began to be stern. He knew the Egyptian language. He was a prime minister. "You men look like thieves to me." he said.

"Oh, no! We are not thieves! We are good men!"

Joseph knew better than that when he was seventeen. He said, "How many children are in your family?"

"Oh, there are ten of us here. One got killed by a wild beast."

"Any more?"

"There is one at home, the youngest one named Benjamin."

He said, "Well, I would like to see him, too. I just want to see if you are honest men."

"Oh, no! Our father has already lost one that he loved very much named Joseph, and he would not trust the other one with us."

"Well," he said, "If you do not bring the other one, then you cannot have any more corn."

On their next trip for corn, they brought young Benjamin in. Joseph could not stand it any longer. He took them to one side and said in their language, "Reuben, Simeon, Levi, Judah . . ."

"You speak our language, sir? You

have understood everything we have said?''

"Yes, I have understood everything you said."

"How do you know our names?"

"Very simple. My name is Joseph!"

"Oh, my God! Now we are all dead!"

Joseph said, "Oh, no, you are not! Let me whisper something to you. You meant it for evil but God meant it for good."

Friend, you can be mistreated and God can turn that sorrow into the best thing that ever happened in your life. Someone can hurt you and that hurt can become the most blessed event of your whole life. Someone can cheat you and that can become the best thing that ever happened to you.

If Joseph had fallen down at any stage of his life, he would have missed the end.

If he had gotten the wrong idea about his father and hated him, or if he had hated his brothers, or if he had hated his cousins who bought him and sold him, or if he had hated Potiphar's wife, or if he had hated the butler in jail, he never would have been the blesser. Haters are never blessed, nor are they blessers. It is the givers that are blessed who can be blessers.

The trajectory of faith means that you begin right, and you also end right!

LANDING ON TARGET

I wish to end my life preaching the gospel. I have preached since I was seventeen years of age, and I wish to preach the same way until I go to heaven. In over fifty years I have not been out of the will of God. I preach what I was taught in Sunday School and have lived as my mother taught me. She said, "Son, be a good man, a clean man, a holy man, and live right." I said, "Yes, I promise!"

It is not just the beginning of your life; it is the end that really counts.

Joseph forgave his brothers. He said, "You did not mean it to bless me, but God did." It does not matter what other people want to do to you; it is what God wants to do to you that is important. Nobody can stop you from doing what God wants you to do.

The trajectory of faith can propel you through life, from birth to death.

Jesus said, "...Be thou faithful unto death, and I will give thee a crown of life" (Revelation 2:10).

Appendix
Joseph, A Type Of Christ
30 Ways

JOSEPH	JESUS
1. Loved by his father. Gen 37:3	"...This is my beloved Son..." Matt. 3:17
2. Hated by his brothers. Gen. 37:4	"...they...hated both me and my father." John 15:24
3. Brothers did not believe him. Gen. 37:8	"...neither did his brethren believe in him." John 7:5
4. Brothers rejected his reign. Gen. 37:20	"...We will not have this man to reign over us." Luke 19:14
5. Brothers conspired against him to slay him." Gen. 37:18	"...took counsel against Jesus to put him to death." Matt. 27:1
6. Mocked. Gen. 37:19	"...after that they had mocked him..." Matt. 27:31
7. Stripped of his coat. Gen. 37:23	"And they stripped him..." Matt. 27:28

8. Sold for silver. Gen. 37:28

   "...and they (sold Him) for thirty pieces of silver." Matt. 26:15

9. All that he did, prospered in his hand. Gen. 39:3

   "...the pleasure of the Lord shall prosper in his hand." Isa. 53:10

10. All things were put into his hand. Gen. 39:4-8

    "The Father...hath given all things into his hand." John 3:35

11. Tempted, but did not sin. Gen. 39:9

    "...tempted like as we are, yet without sin." Heb. 4:15

12. Bound and imprisoned...Gen. 39:20

    "...bound him and they led him away..." Matt. 27:2

13. ...with two malefactors. Gen. 40:2

    "And there were also two other, malefactors,... with him." Luke 23:32

14. One received the message of life, but the other died. Gen. 40:21-22

    "...Today shalt thou be with me in paradise." Luke 23:43

15. None so discreet and wise. Gen. 41:39

    "In whom are hid all the treasures of wisdom and knowledge." Col. 2:3

16. They bowed their knee to him. Gen. 41:43

"...every knee should bow..." Phil. 2:10

17. Thirty years old when service began. Gen. 41:46

Thirty years old when ministry began. Luke 3:23.

18. God used his suffering to save others. Gen. 50:20

God used Christ's suffering to bring salvation. Rom. 5:8.

19. Given power over all Egypt. Gen. 41:4

"...All power is given unto me..." Matt. 28:18

20. Gentile bride to share his glory. Gen. 41:45

"Bride of Christ to share his glory forever." John 14:1-3 NS

21. God promised him a place of authority. Gen. 37:6-7

"...the government shall be upon his shoulder..." Isa. 9:6

22. Cast into a pit, but delivered out of it. Gen. 37:24-28

"Now that he ascended, what is it but that he also descended first into the lower parts of the earth?" Eph. 4:9

23. Imprisoned on false charges. Gen. 39:17-20

"For many are false witness against him..." Mark 14:56

24. His dealings with brothers brought them to repentance. Gen. 50:18

"Now when the centurion and they that were with him, watching Jesus, saw the earthquake, and those things that were done, they feared greatly, saying, Truly this was the Son of God." Matt. 27:54

25. Joseph revealed himself to his brothers during their imprisonment. Gen.45:1

"...by which also he... preached unto the spirits in prison." I Pet. 3:19

26. Taken to Egypt by somebody else. Gen. 37:28

"...he took the young child and his mother by night, and departed into Egypt." Matt. 2:14

27. Joseph wept. Gen. 42:24

"Jesus wept." John 11:35

28. He had compassion. Gen. 45:5

"...He was moved with compassion..." Matt. 9:36 .

29. Told them not to
    fear. Gen. 50:19

    Told his disciples
    not to fear.
    Luke 12:32

30. Forgave them and
    reinstated them to
    position of author-
    ity. Gen. 50:21.

    Forgave them and
    reinstated them to
    position of author-
    ity. Luke 24:47-49 NS

MY CHALLENGE TO YOU

If you are not a Christian, I invite you to receive the hope and peace in your heart that only Jesus gives.

To become a Christian, you must deal with Christ Jesus directly. In a quiet moment, bow your head and talk to Him. In your own words say something like this:

"Dear Lord Jesus, I am a sinner. I believe that you died and rose from the dead to save me from my sins. I want to be with you in heaven forever. God forgive me of all my sins that I have committed against you. I here and now open my heart to you and ask you to come into my heart and life and be my personal Saviour. Amen."

If you say that to Christ and mean it, He will come in instantly. At once you will sense you have been transferred from the devil's dominion to God's kingdom.

Read I John 1:9 and Colossians 1:13. A wonderful peace and joy will fill your soul.

If you pray a prayer like this, let me hear from you. I will send you a little pamphlet entitled, "So You're Born Again!"

Mail your letter to: **Lester Sumrall, P.O. Box 12, South Bend, IN 46624.**

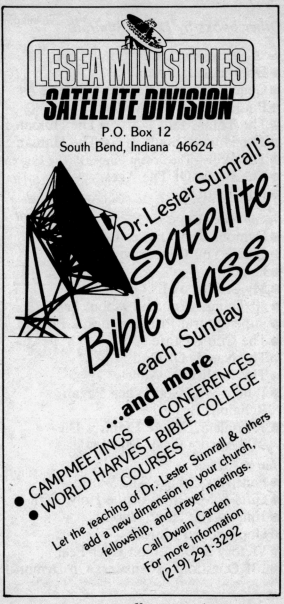

Other books by Lester Sumrall:

☐ My payment for $_____ is enclosed
☐ CHECK   ☐ VISA   ☐ MASTERCARD

SIGNATURE OF CARDHOLDER _____

INTERBANK NUMBER _____/_____/_____ EXPIRATION DATE

_____/_____/_____/_____
CREDIT CARD NUMBER

NAME _____

STREET _____

CITY _____ STATE _____

ZIP_____ PHONE_____

☐ My payment for $_____ is enclosed
☐ CHECK   ☐ VISA   ☐ MASTERCARD

SIGNATURE OF CARDHOLDER _____

INTERBANK NUMBER _____/_____/_____ EXPIRATION DATE

_____/_____/_____/_____
CREDIT CARD NUMBER

NAME _____

STREET _____

CITY _____ STATE _____

ZIP_____ PHONE_____

☐ My payment for $_____ is enclosed
☐ CHECK   ☐ VISA   ☐ MASTERCARD

SIGNATURE OF CARDHOLDER _____

INTERBANK NUMBER _____/_____/_____ EXPIRATION DATE

_____/_____/_____/_____
CREDIT CARD NUMBER

NAME _____

STREET _____

CITY _____ STATE _____

ZIP_____ PHONE_____

**24-Hour Prayer Phone
(219) 291-1010**